SALLY'S CANDY ADDICTION

Tasty Truffles, Fudges & Treats for Your Sweet-Tooth Fix

Race Point
PUBLISHING

Quarto is the authority on a wide range of topics.

Quarto educates, entertains and enriches the lives of
our readers—enthusiasts and lovers of hands-on living.

www.quartoknows.com

First published in the United States of America in 2015 by
Race Point Publishing, a member of
Quarto Publishing Group USA Inc.
142 West 36th Street, 4th Floor
New York, NY 10018
Telephone: (212)779-4972
Fax: (212)779-6058
quartoknows.com
Visit our blogs at quartoknows.com

10 9 8 7 6 5 4 3 2

ISBN: 978-1-63106-031-1

Library of Congress Cataloging-in-Publication Data is available

Editorial Director: Jeannine Dillon
Managing Editor: Erin Canning
Project Editor: Hallie Einhorn
Designer: Heidi North

Printed in China

SALLY'S CANDY ADDICTION

Tasty Truffles, Fudges & Treats for Your Sweet-Tooth Fix

SALLY McKENNEY
Sprinkle Lover & Founder of SallysBakingAddiction.com

DEDICATION

To my blog readers.
Especially those of you who encourage sprinkles and more chocolate.
You made this happen for me.

CONTENTS

ACKNOWLEDGMENTS

Creating this cookbook was challenging, yet exciting. And I could not have done it alone. Thank you to the entire Race Point Publishing crew for helping me produce a second cookbook that I feel is the perfect sequel. Thank you especially to Jeannine Dillon, Hallie Einhorn, Heidi North, Katie Fawkes, Erin Canning, and Becky Gissel. We make one sweet (get it?) cookbook team!

Thank you to my friends and family. You've all done this process with me before and you continued to show the same level of support with my second book. Mom, you are my favorite taste-tester. Your very excited, smiley-face text messages about Caramel Turtles (see page 94) and Caramel Apples (see page 96) made chapter

5 very fun to write. Dad, thank you for all your advice and for pushing me to be the very best I can be. Thank you especially to Sarah, Saundra, the entire Quinn family, Kristen, Amy, Marie, Molly, Kristin, Erin, and Jess. And thank you, Katy, for your endless encouragement and glasses of wine!

Thank you to my readers!! (I want to use about a thousand exclamation points here.) You're my favorite people on the planet. Your sweet teeth and constant excitement about cookbook #2 made it easier to write. You told me your favorite candies, which helped me create the table of contents. Not only this, you've made my blog, Sally's Baking Addiction, a fun-filled community. Please never stop being you! Can I say I love you here? Because I love you.

And finally, thank you to my husband, Kevin. Thank you for all those late nights manning the stove, stirring caramel, toffee, and fudge while I wrote blog posts. I'm sure learning how to properly make toffee was the first thing on your list after marrying me. Thank you for doing all the dishes even after working all day, for your daily emergency grocery store runs, for taste-testing every single recipe, and for smiling through it all. But most of all? Thank you for believing in me when I felt like giving up.

—Sally

INTRODUCTION

There is sticky goop on my hands, sugar all over the floor, and I'm pretty sure I just bought out every single bar of Ghirardelli® chocolate from all the grocery stores within a five-mile radius. It's early December and I'm making dozens of holiday candies to gift this year. As I cook my seventh batch of fudge, I'm beginning to rethink this whole "only homemade gifts this year!" plan.

Welcome to my candy land. It's sort of like my baking addiction, but there's not as much oven involved. Here we trade flour for sugar, and the milk for heavy cream, and instead of a batch of cookies, we'll bond over a batch of chocolate-covered caramels. Oh, there are cookies, too. Wait until you hit the last chapter of this book.

I chose candy as the subject for my second cookbook because, well, truthfully, it scared me a little. How do you use a candy thermometer? What is the correct temperature for heating chocolate? Is there a right method for taffy pulling? Wait, what is taffy pulling? The candy world can be an intimidating place. I felt like I needed a sugar PhD just to get through one batch of fudge. But then I remembered that I was also scared the day I decided to quit my "safe" day job in finance so I could pursue my blog full time. Okay, maybe I was terrified. But I did it, and I never looked back. And guess what? It was the best decision I ever made.

Like blogging, candy making wasn't always easy for me. In fact, I felt like making candy was nearly impossible and left me feeling defeated. When I began several years ago, I quickly became frustrated at the lack of instructional detail and troubleshooting tips. Um, hello? The world was practically screaming for an easy candy-making book! That's when I decided to take matters into my own hands. I dove headfirst into candy land and began teaching myself through experience, advice from my peers, and plenty of mistakes. I burned pans, seized pounds of chocolate, lost a rubber spatula in The Great 2010 Melt (let's not talk about it), and made some funky brittle substance that nearly broke my teeth. My dentist loves that story.

I understand that the thought of candy making can be overwhelming. I get it, I've been there. But I wrote this book to help give you the confidence to make candy from scratch. If you want to learn how to make chewy taffy for your children, smooth truffles for a bake sale, old-fashioned fudge for your grandchildren, caramels for your friends, and chocolates for your sweetheart, let me help you. I've cooked my way through batches of toffee just so I can tell you what NOT to do. And, well, so I'd be able to eat really delicious homemade toffee. Please refer to the toffee goodness on pages 104–111.

On the next few pages, you'll find information about key ingredients, essential equipment, and important candy-making basics. But I don't stop there! Sprinkled throughout the book are several how-tos and tricks to help build your candy-making confidence. Avoid disasters in the kitchen by taking the time to read my tips. These few minutes could save you from losing your mind, or worse, losing a spatula.

As for me, I'm proud to say that four years, three pea-size kitchens, and a wedding later, my blog is still my full-time job and it's better than ever. I've built up the courage and knowledge to connect with millions of readers. And I wouldn't trade it for the world. So do something that scares you. Maybe it will change your life. Maybe you'll get a little more confident in the kitchen. Maybe you'll get more confident in other parts of your life. Or maybe you'll just get to eat some home-made Lemon Cream Pie Truffles (see page 88).

The most important thing you need to know about making candy? Have fun. It's candy!

BUTTER RUM HARD CANDIES

Prep time: 40 minutes
Total time: 1 hour
Makes: 117 x 1-in (2.5cm) candies

INGREDIENTS

2 cups (400g) sugar

½ cup (110g) light brown sugar, packed

¾ cup (180ml) water

½ cup (120ml) light corn syrup

1 cup (2 sticks; 227g) unsalted butter, softened to room temperature and cut into 16 pieces

¼ cup (60ml) honey

¾ tsp salt

½ tsp rum extract

SPECIAL EQUIPMENT

9 x 13-in (23 x 33cm) baking pan

3-qt (2.8L) heavy-duty saucepan

candy thermometer

pastry brush

dough scraper or sharp serrated knife

wax paper or cellophane for wrapping

These creamy and comforting butter rum candies prove that you don't always need chocolate to satisfy your sweet tooth. Made from familiar ingredients, such as brown sugar, butter, and honey, the secret to this candy's scrumptious flavor is rum extract. You quickly stir it in after the candy reaches the hard crack stage at 300°F (149°C), and that's when the magic happens. Somehow word spreads fast whenever I make a batch of these sweets (I'm looking at you, Mom), and I get knocks at the door from everyone looking to sneak a taste. How can I say no?

1   Line a 9 x 13-in (23 x 33cm) baking pan with parchment paper. Set aside.

2   Place the sugar, brown sugar, water, and corn syrup in a 3-qt (2.8L) heavy-duty saucepan over medium heat. Stir with a wooden spoon until the sugar is dissolved. Attach a candy thermometer to the pan. Remember not to let it touch the bottom of the pan. As the mixture begins cooking, brush down the sides of the pan with a water-moistened pastry brush.

3   Once boiling, stop stirring. Cook the candy until it reaches 270°F (132°C; soft crack stage). Quickly stir in the butter, honey, and salt. The candy's temperature will temporarily drop. While lightly stirring, cook the candy until it reaches 300°F (149°C; hard crack stage). Turn the stove off and remove the pan from heat. Stir in the rum extract and pour the candy into the prepared pan. Allow to cool for 3–5 minutes. Using a dough scraper or sharp serrated knife, score the candy into 1-in (2.5cm) squares while it is still semisoft. Allow the candy to cool completely, then separate and break into squares.

MAKE-AHEAD TIP: To really make the candies last, wrap each piece individually in a wax paper or cellophane square—you can either cut your own or purchase premade wrappers online or at candy supply shops (see photo, opposite). Store wrapped candies at room temperature in a cool, dry place for up to 1 month.

POPCORN BALLS

Prep time: 25 minutes
Total time: 40 minutes
Makes: 10 balls

INGREDIENTS

5 tbsp unsalted butter, softened to room temperature, divided (plus more for greasing)

8 cups (64g) air-popped popcorn

1 cup (200g) sugar

⅓ cup (80ml) light corn syrup

⅓ cup (80ml) water

1 tsp distilled white vinegar

1 tsp salt

1 tsp vanilla extract

SPECIAL EQUIPMENT

large baking sheet

3-qt (2.8L) heavy-duty saucepan

candy thermometer

pastry brush

The first idea I wrote down as I brainstormed the table of contents for this book was popcorn balls. My grandparents made these treats every Halloween. Working as a team, my grandpa popped the popcorn and my grandma prepared the sugar syrup. Together, they rolled the combined mixture into balls. I'm not sure if it was the sweet and salty taste, the satisfying chewy texture, or the fact that they made the treats together, but my grandparents loved the fruits of their labor. I can't bite into one without remembering them both. Here is their recipe.

1   Line a large baking sheet with parchment paper or a silicone baking mat.

2   Coat a large heatproof bowl with 1 tablespoon (14g) of the butter. Add the popcorn. Set the bowl and the remaining butter aside.

3   Place the sugar, salt, corn syrup, water, and white vinegar in a 3-qt (2.8L) heavy-duty saucepan over medium heat. Stir with a wooden spoon until the sugar has dissolved. There is no more stirring beyond this point as the candy cooks. Attach a candy thermometer to the pan. Remember not to let it touch the bottom of the pan. As the mixture begins cooking, brush down the sides of the pan with a water-moistened pastry brush.

4   Cook the candy until it reaches 260°F (127°C; hard ball stage). Turn the stove off and immediately remove the pan from heat. Stir in the remaining butter and the vanilla until smooth.

5   Pour the candy over the popcorn and, using a rubber spatula, stir until all of the popcorn is coated. Make sure you scrape the sides of the bowl to really get all of the candy mixture onto the popcorn. Allow to slightly cool for a minute. Then, using buttered hands, form sticky popcorn into tight 3-in (7.5cm) balls. Place balls on prepared baking sheet and allow to cool completely before serving.

MAKE-AHEAD TIP: Once the balls have cooled, wrap each individually in plastic wrap and store for up to 3–4 days at room temperature in a cool, dry place.

"pulling taffy is like weight lifting!"

SALTWATER TAFFY

Prep time: 50 minutes
Total time: 1 hour, 40 minutes
Makes: 50 pieces

INGREDIENTS

2 tbsp butter, plus more for greasing

2 cups (400g) sugar

2 tbsp (16g) cornstarch

1 cup (240ml) light corn syrup

¾ cup (180ml) water

1 tsp salt

flavoring (see *Sally Says*, below)

1–2 drops liquid food coloring (optional)

SPECIAL EQUIPMENT

12 x 17-in (30 x 43cm) jelly roll pan or a similar-sized rimmed baking sheet

silicone baking mat (recommended)

3-qt (2.8L) heavy-duty saucepan

candy thermometer

pastry brush

kitchen shears

wax paper for wrapping

SALLY SAYS: Flavoring oils or pure flavored extracts (not imitation) are best for taffy. I recommend ½ teaspoon LorAnn Oils or 1 teaspoon McCormick® pure extracts per batch. The flavors pictured here are vanilla, peppermint, strawberry, and orange.

Saltwater taffy is one of the best parts of a beach vacation. We used to come home with boxes of it—none of which lasted more than a few days! Taffy must be cooked to a precise temperature to achieve the perfect chewy texture. Undercooking will give it a soft, unworkable consistency; overcooking will yield a candy too hard to be called taffy. After it cooks, taffy must be pulled to get that volume. I'm warning you though, pulling taffy is as tough as lifting weights—that's why candy shops use machines!

1   Butter a 12 x 17-in (30 x 43cm) jelly roll pan. Place in the refrigerator to chill as you prepare the taffy. A nonstick surface for cutting the taffy is needed. I use and strongly suggest a silicone baking mat. Parchment or wax paper works as well. Have it ready on your counter.

2   Whisk sugar and cornstarch together in a 3-qt (2.8L) heavy-duty saucepan. Place over medium heat and add the corn syrup, water, butter, and salt. Stir with a wooden spoon as the sugar dissolves. Attach a candy thermometer to the pan. Remember not to let it touch the bottom of the pan. As the mixture begins cooking, brush down the sides of the pan with a water-moistened pastry brush.

3   Once boiling, stop stirring. Cook the candy until it reaches 250°F (121°C; hard ball stage). Turn the stove off and remove the pan from heat. Remove the jelly roll pan from the refrigerator. Allow the candy to cool down to 240°F (116°C; soft ball stage) and gently stir in the flavoring and coloring of choice. Without scraping the pan, immediately pour the candy onto the prepared jelly roll pan and allow to slightly cool until you are comfortable handling the taffy. I usually wait around 8 minutes.

4   After the candy is cool enough to handle, lightly butter your hands and begin to pull the taffy (if you put too much butter on your hands, the taffy will begin to separate). I like to work with only half of the taffy at a time. Grab a friend and have her pull the other half. To pull the taffy, stretch the ends out from the middle and then fold them back toward the center. Repeat this process for about 15 minutes, until the taffy lightens and becomes more elastic. The taffy will be sticky.

5   When it is ready, place the taffy on the nonstick surface prepared in step 1. Butter a pair of kitchen shears and cut off a piece of taffy. Roll the piece into a rope, about ½ inch (1.25cm) in diameter, and cut it into pieces 2 inches (5cm) in length. Wrap the individual pieces in wax paper soon after they have been cut to prevent sticking. Repeat with remaining taffy.

MAKE-AHEAD TIP: Store wrapped taffy at room temperature in a cool, dry place for up to 2 weeks. For longer storage, freeze for up to 2 months. Thaw in the refrigerator before serving.

PEANUT BUTTER CUPS

Prep time: 30 minutes
Total time: 45 minutes
Makes: 36 cups

INGREDIENTS

1 cup (258g) creamy peanut butter, divided

1 tbsp unsalted butter, softened to room temperature

½ cup (60g) confectioners' sugar

½ tsp salt

3 cups (546g) milk chocolate chips

chocolate sprinkles (optional)

SPECIAL EQUIPMENT

2 x 24-count mini muffin pans

36 mini muffin/cupcake liners

handheld or stand mixer fitted with a paddle attachment

You've hit one of the best recipes in this entire book—HOMEMADE PEANUT BUTTER CUPS. Enough said.

1   Line two 24-count mini muffin pans with mini liners (the second pan will need only 12 liners since this recipe makes 36 cups). Set aside.

2   With a handheld or stand mixer fitted with a paddle attachment, beat ½ cup (129g) of the peanut butter, butter, confectioners' sugar, and salt on medium speed in a medium-size bowl until thick and smooth, about 3 minutes. You will be tempted to add milk because the mixture will be crumbly, but do not. Just keep mixing until it comes together. Set aside.

3   Combine the chocolate chips with the remaining ½ cup (129g) of peanut butter in a medium heatproof bowl. Melt in the microwave on 50 percent power in 20-second increments, stirring after each increment, until completely smooth and melted. Drop 1 teaspoon of chocolate–peanut butter mixture into each mini muffin cup. Next, measure out a scant teaspoon of the peanut butter–sugar mixture and roll it into a ball with your hands, slightly flattening it into a small, thick disc. Place on top of the chocolate–peanut butter mixture. Repeat to make the rest of the cups. Top each with another teaspoon of the chocolate–peanut butter mixture. Decorate with sprinkles, if desired. Once all of the peanut butter cups have been assembled, refrigerate for 15 minutes, or until chocolate has completely set.

MAKE-AHEAD TIP: It's best to keep the peanut butter cups in their liners when storing. Layer them between sheets of parchment or wax paper in an airtight container and store in the refrigerator for up to 1 week or in the freezer for up to 2 months.

 SALLY SAYS: I don't normally suggest melting chocolate chips as coating for candies, but for this recipe, it works! Melting them down with peanut butter helps thin out their consistency. You can easily use semi-sweet chocolate chips instead of milk chocolate. I like to use milk chocolate because it makes the peanut butter cups taste like the real deal.

CHOCOLATE-DIPPED PRETZELS

Prep time: 45 mi...
Total time: 1 ho...
Makes: ½ poun...

Ingredients

- 14oz (397g) semi-sweet chocolate, coarsely chopped
- 8oz (227g) pretzel twists, divided
- 14oz (397g) white chocolate, coarsely chopped
- sprinkles (optional)

Special Equipment

- 3 large baking sheets
- double boiler (optional)
- 2 squeeze bottles (optional)

Chocolate-dipped pretzels are w...
I couldn't write a candy cookbo...
favorite that I've been making f...
prepare any other kind of des...
using white and semi-sweet...
this recipe. Don't forget to...
sprinkles. Clearly, they're...

1 Line 3 large baking sheets with parchmen...
  Set aside.

2 Melt or temper the semi-sweet chocolate (see page 42). Dip a pretze...
  quarters of the way into the warm chocolate, lift it out of the chocolate, and
  gently shake it to allow excess chocolate to drip off. Place pretzel onto the
  prepared baking sheet to allow chocolate to set. Repeat with half of the
  pretzels. If decorating with sprinkles, do so while the chocolate is still wet.

3 Melt or temper the white chocolate and dip the remaining pretzels into the
  warm white chocolate as you did in step 2.

4 Optional: If you want to add an extra chocolate drizzle to the pretzels (as
  pictured here), warm any leftover semi-sweet and/or white chocolate in the
  double boiler—or in small heatproof bowls in the microwave at 50 percent
  power for 10 seconds each. Drizzle white chocolate over pretzels dipped in
  semi-sweet chocolate, and semi-sweet chocolate over those dipped in white
  chocolate with squeeze bottles (or forks).

5 Allow chocolate to completely set before serving, about 30 minutes.

MAKE-AHEAD TIP: If the chocolate hasn't been tempered, wrap pretzels
tightly in plastic wrap and store in an airtight container in the refrigerator
for up to 2 weeks. If the chocolate has been tempered, wrap and store
pretzels in an airtight container at room temperature in a cool, dry place for
up to 4 weeks.

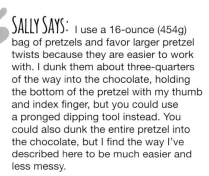

Sally Says: I use a 16-ounce (454g) bag of pretzels and favor larger pretzel twists because they are easier to work with. I dunk them about three-quarters of the way into the chocolate, holding the bottom of the pretzel with my thumb and index finger, but you could use a pronged dipping tool instead. You could also dunk the entire pretzel into the chocolate, but I find the way I've described here to be much easier and less messy.

ED COCOA MARSHMALLOWS

Prep time: 50 minutes
Total time: 7 hours, 50 minutes
Makes: about 58 x 2-in (5cm) marshmallows

natural unsweetened
process cocoa powder,

p (30g) confectioners' sugar

tbsp (16g) cornstarch

1⅓ cups (320ml) cold water, divided

3 x ¼oz (7g) package unflavored
gelatin

1 cup (240ml) light corn syrup

1½ cups (300g) sugar

¼ tsp salt

1 tsp vanilla extract

16oz (454g) semi-sweet chocolate,
coarsely chopped

chocolate sprinkles

Special Equipment

9 x 13-in (23 x 33cm) glass or
ceramic baking pan

stand mixer fitted with a whisk
attachment

3-qt (2.8L) heavy-duty saucepan

candy thermometer

pastry brush

2 large baking sheets

double boiler (optional)

These cocoa marshmallows are the perfect addition to a steamy mug of hot chocolate on a cold winter afternoon. They begin the same way as my Marshmallows (see page 20), but I simply add a cocoa mixture to the gelatin before pouring in the cooked sugar syrup for that wonderful cocoa flavor. These sweets make a wonderful gift for the chocoholic in your life . . . just don't forget the chocolate sprinkles!

1 Generously spray the bottom and sides of a 9 x 13-in (23 x 33cm) glass or ceramic baking pan with nonstick cooking spray. Set aside. Sift half of the cocoa powder (⅓ cup, or 28g), the confectioners' sugar, and the cornstarch together in a small bowl and very lightly sprinkle all around the prepared pan. Leave enough to use in steps 8 and 9, and set aside.

2 Place remaining cocoa powder and ⅓ cup (80ml) water in a heatproof bowl or mug. Microwave on high power for 90 seconds. Stir the hot mixture vigorously until combined. Set aside.

3 Place gelatin and ½ cup (120ml) water in the bowl of a stand mixer fitted with a whisk attachment. Whisk on low speed for 1 minute to briefly combine. Add the hot cocoa mixture and whisk on low speed for 30 seconds. Allow to sit as you begin cooking the sugar syrup.

4 Place the remaining ½ cup (120ml) water, corn syrup, sugar, and salt in a 3-qt (2.8L) heavy-duty saucepan over medium heat. Stir with a wooden spoon until the sugar is dissolved. Attach a candy thermometer to the pan. Remember not to let it touch the bottom of the pan. As the sugar syrup begins cooking, brush down the sides of the pan with a water-moistened pastry brush to prevent crystallization. Without stirring, cook the sugar syrup until it reaches 240°F (116°C; soft ball stage). In the meantime, every 3 minutes or so, turn the mixer on low for 20 seconds to ensure the gelatin and cocoa mixture remains well mixed.

5 Turn the stove off and remove the pan with the sugar syrup from heat. Turn the mixer on low speed and slowly pour the hot syrup into the gelatin mixture. The syrup is extremely hot, so be careful.

6 Gradually increase the mixer speed until it reaches high. Whip the mixture for 10–15 minutes, or until it is light brown, thick, and shiny. During the last minute of mixing, add the vanilla extract.

7 Pour/spoon the marshmallow mixture into the prepared baking pan and smooth out the top with a rubber spatula. Allow it to sit uncovered at room temperature for at least 6 hours, preferably overnight.

8 Once completely firm, it is time to cut the marshmallows. Cover a large workstation with wax or parchment paper. Liberally sprinkle the surface, as well as the top of the marshmallow, with some of the remaining cocoa/

confectioners' sugar/cornstarch mixture. Using a sharp knife, loosen the edges of the marshmallow from the pan and invert the pan onto the prepared surface. Lift a corner of the pan and use your fingers to help peel the marshmallow away from the pan.

9   Using a sharp knife, cut the marshmallow into 2-in (5cm) squares, coating the knife blade with some of the remaining cocoa/confectioners' sugar/cornstarch mixture as needed. I find running the blade under hot water and wiping dry with a paper towel helps make clean cuts as well. Roll the cut edges of the marshmallows in the coating mixture so they are no longer sticky.

10 Line 2 large baking sheets with parchment paper or silicone baking mats. Set aside. Melt or temper the semi-sweet chocolate (see page 42). Dip a marshmallow halfway into the warm chocolate, lift it out of the chocolate, and gently shake it to allow excess chocolate to drip off. Place marshmallow onto the prepared baking sheet and top with sprinkles. Repeat with remaining marshmallows. Allow chocolate to completely set before serving.

MAKE-AHEAD TIP: If you don't eat the marshmallows immediately, layer them between sheets of parchment or wax paper in an airtight container and store at room temperature in a cool, dry place for up to 1 week.

CHOCOLATE-DIPPED POTATO CHIPS

Prep time: 25 minutes
Total time: 40 minutes (includes chilling)
Makes: 8 servings

Ingredients

12oz (340g) semi-sweet chocolate, coarsely chopped

16oz (454g) bag thick-ridged potato chips

sprinkles

Special Equipment

2 large baking sheets

double boiler (optional)

My friends invited me over to watch Sunday football recently (which to me means sitting and eating on the couch with the game on somewhere in the background), and they asked me to bring chips and dip. So, I brought these. What? Don't look at me like that. There are chips. And there's dip. And I'm happy to report that these chocolate-covered potato chips disappeared before the first beer was popped open. Touchdown . . . for real.

1   Line 2 large baking sheets with parchment paper or silicone baking mats. Set aside.

2   Melt or temper the semi-sweet chocolate (see page 42), then immediately begin dipping chips. Simply hold a chip by one end and dip it halfway into the chocolate. Lightly tap the chip on the edge of the bowl holding the chocolate to remove excess. Place the dipped chip onto prepared baking sheet and immediately top the chocolate with sprinkles while still wet. Repeat with remaining chips. Allow chocolate to completely set before serving.

MAKE-AHEAD TIP: It is not a good idea to make this recipe in advance, as over time, the chips start to lose their crunch. Instead, serve them soon after they are dipped. Keep them at room temperature.

SALLY SAYS: You won't use the entire bag of potato chips because there are always broken chips that are difficult to coat in chocolate. You should crush up the leftover broken chips and use them as decoration for Caramel Apples (page 96). No really. Try it.

PEANUT BUTTER BUCKEYES

Prep time: 30 minutes
Total time: 1 hour (includes chilling)
Makes: 32 balls

Ingredients

½ cup (1 stick; 114g) unsalted butter, softened to room temperature

¾ cup (194g) creamy peanut butter (not natural style)

½ tsp vanilla extract

⅛ tsp salt

3 cups (360g) confectioners' sugar

16oz (454g) semi-sweet chocolate

Special Equipment

2 large baking sheets

handheld or stand mixer fitted with a paddle attachment

double boiler (optional)

dipping tool (optional)

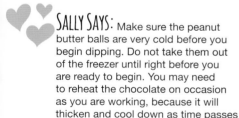

Sally Says: Make sure the peanut butter balls are very cold before you begin dipping. Do not take them out of the freezer until right before you are ready to begin. You may need to reheat the chocolate on occasion as you are working, because it will thicken and cool down as time passes during the dipping process.

What the heck is a buckeye?! I didn't just make up that name, I swear. Buckeyes are peanut butter balls partially dipped in semi-sweet chocolate. They're practically the same thing as peanut butter cups (page 32), just in a different shape. My friend Marie, who is from Cleveland, Ohio, tells me that they're named for their resemblance to the nut of the Ohio buckeye tree. Whatever they're called, they're fan-freaking-tastic. (That word is really the only way to describe them.) I do not recommend tempered chocolate for this recipe, as the peanut butter filling tastes best stored in the refrigerator.

1 Line 2 large baking sheets with parchment paper or silicone baking mats. Set aside.

2 Using a handheld or stand mixer fitted with a paddle attachment, beat the butter on medium speed in a large bowl until creamy, about 2 minutes. Add the peanut butter, vanilla, and salt. Beat on high until combined and creamy. Add the confectioners' sugar and beat on low for 2 minutes until everything is combined. The mixture is supposed to be a little soft, yet crumbly (see inset photo).

3 Begin rolling peanut butter dough into 1-in (2.5cm) balls and place on the baking sheets.

4 Chill peanut butter balls in the freezer until firm, about 30 minutes, or in the refrigerator for 1 hour. During the last few minutes of the chilling time, begin melting the chocolate. Melt the chocolate, being careful not to overheat it (see page 44).

5 Remove peanut butter balls from the freezer or refrigerator and dip them in the chocolate using a dipping tool (or fork). When dipping, leave a small portion of peanut butter showing at the top to make them look like buckeyes. When lifting the buckeye out of the chocolate, remember to tap the dipping tool gently on the side of the bowl to allow excess chocolate to drip off.

6 Place balls, peanut-butter side up, back onto the baking sheet after you dip each one. Allow chocolate to completely set before serving.

MAKE-AHEAD TIP: Layer buckeyes between sheets of parchment or wax paper in an airtight container in the refrigerator for up to 1 week or in the freezer for up to 2 months. Thaw overnight in the refrigerator.

EASY VANILLA BUTTERCREAMS

Prep time: 30 minutes
Total time: 1 hour
Makes: 60 candies

Ingredients

½ cup (1 stick; 114g) unsalted butter, softened to room temperature

4 cups (480g) confectioners' sugar

3 tbsp (44ml) heavy cream

1 tbsp (15ml) vanilla extract

20oz (567g) semi-sweet chocolate, coarsely chopped

4oz (113g) white chocolate, coarsely chopped

Special Equipment

2 large baking sheets

double boiler (optional)

handheld or stand mixer fitted with a paddle attachment

dipping tool (optional)

squeeze bottle (optional)

 Sally Says: Make sure the buttercreams are very cold before you begin dipping—it makes the process much easier.

American poet Robert Frost once said, "In three words, I can sum up everything I've learned in life: it goes on." Absolutely true. Another trio of words I find significant: frosting rules all. Vanilla buttercream candies are basically chocolate-covered frosting. Delicious? Yes. Sweet? Irresistible? Oh yes. For an equally easy fruity treat, see my strawberry version on page 56! I do not recommend tempered chocolate for this recipe, and the buttercream tastes best refrigerated.

1   Line 2 large baking sheets with parchment paper or silicone baking mats. Set aside.

2   Using a handheld or stand mixer fitted with a paddle attachment, beat the butter on medium speed in a large bowl until creamy, about 2 minutes. Add the confectioners' sugar and beat on low for 1 minute. Add the cream and vanilla and beat on high for 3 minutes, or until completely smooth and creamy. The mixture will be very sticky. Cover the bowl tightly with aluminum foil or plastic wrap and chill in the refrigerator for at least 1 hour and up to 1 day. Chilling for the short period of time makes working with the buttercream a little easier.

3   Once chilled, remove the mixture from the refrigerator. Scoop 1 teaspoon of the buttercream mixture and roll into a ball. Slightly flatten the ball with your hands and place on prepared baking sheet. Repeat with rest of buttercream mixture. As you are rolling, if the mixture starts to become too soft to handle, chill in the refrigerator for 15 minutes. To help prevent the buttercream from sticking to your hands, powder your hands with confectioners' sugar.

4   Chill the buttercreams in the refrigerator for at least 1 hour and up to 1 day. During the last few minutes of the chilling time, melt the chocolate (see page 44).

5   Remove buttercreams from the refrigerator and dip each one completely into the chocolate using a dipping tool (or fork). I like to use a spoon or fork in addition to the dipping tool to help coat the buttercream when it is submerged in the chocolate. When lifting the buttercream out of the chocolate, remember to tap the dipping tool gently on the side of the bowl to allow excess chocolate to drip off. Place buttercreams back onto baking sheet after dipping.

6   Melt the white chocolate (see page 44). Remove from heat and drizzle over buttercreams with a squeeze bottle (or fork). Refrigerate for 15 minutes, or until chocolate has completely set, before serving.

MAKE-AHEAD TIP: Layer buttercreams between sheets of parchment or wax paper and store in an airtight container in the refrigerator for up to 2 weeks. For longer storage, freeze for up to 2 months and thaw overnight in the refrigerator.

STRAWBERRY BUTTERCREAMS

Prep time: 30 minu
Total time: 1 hour
Makes: 60 candies

INGREDIENTS

1 cup (20g) freeze-dried strawberries

½ cup (1 stick; 114g) unsalted butter, softened to room temperature

3½ cups (420g) confectioners' sugar

3 tbsp (44g) heavy cream

2 tsp vanilla extract

20oz (567g) bittersweet chocolate, coarsely chopped

4oz (113g) pink candy coating (see page 13)

SPECIAL EQUIPMENT

food processor or blender

2 large baking sheets

handheld or stand mixer fitted with a paddle attachment

double boiler (optional)

dipping tool (optional)

squeeze bottle (optional)

Here is an elegant collision of two
frosting and bittersweet chocolate
chocolate candies is similar to Ea
For a brilliant strawberry flavor, I
into powder using a food proces
with butter, confectioners' suga
guaranteed a (pink!) recipe for

1 Using a food processor or blender, grind up the
into a fine powder. There should be around ½ cup of powder tot

2 Line 2 large baking sheets with parchment paper or silicone baking mats. Set aside.

3 With a handheld or stand mixer fitted with a paddle attachment, beat the butter on medium speed in a large bowl until creamy, about 2 minutes. Add the confectioners' sugar and ½ cup of strawberry powder and beat on low for 1 minute. Add the cream and vanilla and beat on high for 3 minutes, or until completely smooth and creamy. The mixture will be very sticky. Cover the bowl tightly with aluminum foil or plastic wrap and chill in the refrigerator for at least 1 hour and up to 1 day. Chilling for the short period of time makes working with the buttercream a little easier.

4 Once chilled, remove the mixture from the refrigerator. Scoop 1 teaspoon of the buttercream mixture and roll into a ball. Slightly flatten the ball with your hands and place on prepared baking sheet (see photo on page 58). Repeat with rest of buttercream mixture. As you are rolling, if the mixture starts to become too soft to handle, chill in the refrigerator for 15 minutes. To help prevent the buttercream from sticking to your hands, powder your hands with confectioners' sugar.

5 Chill the buttercreams in the refrigerator for at least 1 hour and up to 1 day. During the last few minutes of the chilling time, melt the chocolate (see page 44).

6 Remove buttercreams from the refrigerator and dip each one completely into the chocolate using a dipping tool (or fork). I like to use a spoon or fork in addition to the dipping tool to help coat the buttercream when it is submerged in the chocolate. When lifting the buttercream out of the chocolate, remember to tap the dipping tool gently on the side of the bowl to allow excess chocolate to drip off. Place buttercreams back onto baking sheet after dipping.

continued next page

7   Melt candy coating in a small heatproof bowl in the microwave at 50 percent power in 20-second increments, stirring after each increment, until completely smooth and melted. Remove from heat and drizzle over buttercreams with a squeeze bottle (or fork). Refrigerate for 15 minutes or until chocolate has completely set before serving.

SALLY SAYS: If bittersweet chocolate isn't your favorite, use semi-sweet chocolate instead.

MAKE-AHEAD TIP: Layer buttercreams between sheets of parchment or wax paper and store in an airtight container in the refrigerator for up to 2 weeks. For longer storage, freeze for up to 2 months and thaw overnight in the refrigerator.

CHOCOLATE CRUNCH CANDY BARS

Prep time: 15 minutes
Total time: 1 hour, 15 minutes
Makes: about 18 bars

Ingredients

2 cups (50g) crispy rice cereal

24oz (680g) semi-sweet chocolate, coarsely chopped

Special Equipment

9 x 13-in (23 x 33cm) baking pan

double boiler (optional)

MAKE-AHEAD TIP: I like to wrap each bar individually in plastic wrap for a quick grab 'n' go treat. If chocolate has not been tempered, wrapped candy bars keep well in an airtight container in the refrigerator for up to 10 days. If chocolate has been tempered, wrapped candy bars keep well in an airtight container in a cool, dry place for 3 weeks.

It does not get any easier. The end.

1   Line a 9 x 13-in (23 x 33cm) baking pan with aluminum foil or parchment paper, leaving enough overhang on the sides to easily remove the mixture once the chocolate has set. Set aside.

2   Pour crispy rice cereal into a very large heatproof bowl. Set aside.

3   Melt or temper the semi-sweet chocolate (see page 42), then immediately pour over cereal and stir with a rubber spatula or wooden spoon until combined. Pour mixture into the prepared baking pan and, as best you can, smooth into an even layer. I like to use the back of a small spoon to smooth this bumpy mixture down into the pan. Cover the pan tightly and allow the chocolate to completely set in the refrigerator (if chocolate has not been tempered) or at room temperature (if chocolate has been tempered).

4   Once the chocolate has set, remove the whole mixture from the pan using the overhang on the sides; invert onto a large cutting board, peel away foil, turn back over, and cut into bars.

SIMPLY CHOCOLATE TRUFFLES

Prep time: 1 hour
Total time: 5 hours, 30 minutes
Makes: 60 truffles

FILLING

7oz (198g) bittersweet chocolate, coarsely chopped

7oz (198g) semi-sweet chocolate, coarsely chopped

¾ cup (180ml) heavy cream

½ tsp vanilla extract

2 tbsp unsalted butter, softened to room temperature and quartered

COATING

16oz (454g) semi-sweet chocolate, coarsely chopped

SPECIAL EQUIPMENT

double boiler (optional)

large baking sheet

dipping tool (optional)

Simple and satisfying, these chocolate truffles are beyond belief. They're as creamy as New York cheesecake and as chocolaty as a pan of brownies. Be sure to read all of my tips on page 71 before starting.

1   Make the filling: Place the bittersweet chocolate and semi-sweet chocolate in a large heatproof bowl. Microwave on 50 percent power in four 15-second increments, stirring after each, for a total of 60 seconds. Stir until almost completely melted. Set aside.

2   Pour heavy cream into a small saucepan over medium heat. Whisking occasionally, heat until it just begins to boil. Remove from heat, whisk in the vanilla extract, and pour over the chocolate. Gently begin stirring with a wooden spoon in one direction. Do not forcefully stir. Once the chocolate and cream are completely smooth, gently stir in the butter until melted and combined. Cover with plastic wrap pressed on the top of the mixture. Let sit at room temperature for 30 minutes, then transfer to the refrigerator for 3–4 hours, or just until it reaches scoopable consistency (see photo, below left).

3   Line a large baking sheet with parchment paper or a silicone baking mat. Set aside. Remove ganache from the refrigerator. Measure 1 teaspoon, roll between your hands into a ball, and place on the baking sheet. Repeat with the rest of the ganache. Place the truffles in the refrigerator as you prepare the coating.

4   Make the coating: Melt or temper the semi-sweet chocolate (see page 42).

5   Remove truffles from the refrigerator. Working with one truffle at a time, dip completely into the chocolate using a dipping tool (or fork). Place back onto the baking sheet. Repeat with rest of truffles. Drizzle any leftover melted or tempered chocolate with a squeeze bottle (or fork) over truffles. Allow the chocolate to completely set at room temperature before serving.

MAKE-AHEAD TIP: See *Ahead of the Game* (page 72).

 SALLY SAYS: For dark chocolate truffles, use all bittersweet chocolate.

MINT TRUFFLES

Prep time: 1 hour
Total time: 5 hours, 30 minutes
Makes: 60 truffles

FILLING

14oz (397g) semi-sweet chocolate, coarsely chopped

¾ cup (180ml) heavy cream

1 tsp peppermint extract

2 tbsp unsalted butter, softened to room temperature and quartered

COATING

14oz (397g) white chocolate, coarsely chopped

1 drop green food coloring

6oz (170g) semi-sweet chocolate, coarsely chopped

SPECIAL EQUIPMENT

large baking sheet

double boiler (optional)

dipping tool (optional)

Here we meet chocolate's second so[...] with "p" and ends with "eanut butte[...] ganache filling is similar to that in S[...] except all semi-sweet chocolate is u[...] peppermint extract. The coating is [...] a touch of green food coloring. Th[...] (397g) of green candy coating. Be [...] before starting.

1   Make the filling: Place the semi-sweet chocolate in a large heatproof bowl. Microwave on 50 percent power in four 15-second increments, stirring after each, for a total of 60 seconds. Stir until almost completely melted. Set aside.

2   Pour heavy cream in a small saucepan over medium heat. Whisking occasionally, heat until it just begins to boil. Remove from heat, whisk in the peppermint extract, and pour over the chocolate. Gently begin stirring with a wooden spoon in one direction. Do not forcefully stir. Once the chocolate and cream are completely smooth, gently stir in the butter until melted and combined. Cover with plastic wrap pressed on the top of the mixture. Let sit at room temperature for 30 minutes, then transfer to the refrigerator for 3–4 hours, or just until it reaches scoopable consistency.

3   Line a large baking sheet with parchment paper or a silicone baking mat. Set aside. Remove ganache from the refrigerator. Measure 1 teaspoon, roll between your hands into a ball, and place on the baking sheet. Repeat with the rest of the ganache. Place the truffles in the refrigerator as you prepare the coating.

4   Make the coating: Melt or temper the white chocolate (see page 42). Stir in the food coloring.

5   Remove truffles from the refrigerator. Working with one truffle at a time, dip completely into the white chocolate using a dipping tool (or fork). Place back onto the baking sheet. Repeat with remaining truffles. Melt or temper the semi-sweet chocolate. With a squeeze bottle (or fork) drizzle over truffles. Allow the chocolate to completely set at room temperature before serving.

MAKE-AHEAD TIP: See *Ahead of the Game* (page 72).

SALLY SAYS: Avoid using mint extract; I find it resembles the taste of spearmint toothpaste more than anything else. Peppermint extract has that wonderful cool mint flavor, which pairs perfectly with chocolate.

...ATE MOCHA TRUFFLES

Prep time: 1 hour
Total time: 5 hours, 30 minutes
Makes: 40 truffles

...227g) bittersweet chocolate,
...arsely chopped

¾ cup (180ml) heavy cream

1 tbsp instant coffee granules or 1
tsp instant espresso

½ tsp vanilla extract

COATING

10oz (283g) bittersweet chocolate,
coarsely chopped

6oz (170g) white chocolate, coarsely
chopped

40 coffee beans, for garnish
(optional)

SPECIAL EQUIPMENT

large baking sheet

double boiler (optional)

dipping tool (optional)

For the deepest, darkest chocolate experience, indulge in a couple of these mocha truffles. Cream is heated with instant coffee and then mixed with vanilla extract and bittersweet chocolate to create a rich mocha-flavored ganache. This ganache's smell, by the way, will seduce you. Each truffle is then enveloped in even more chocolate, drizzled with white chocolate, and finished off with a coffee bean (this last touch can be omitted if you prefer). Eating one of these truffles is like wearing a cocktail dress to a casual Wednesday lunch; you can't help but feel fancy.

1   Make the filling: Place bittersweet chocolate in a large heatproof bowl. Microwave on 50 percent power in three 15-second increments, stirring after each, for a total of 45 seconds. Stir until almost completely melted. Set aside.

2   Whisk the heavy cream and instant coffee together in a small saucepan over medium heat. Whisking occasionally, heat until it just begins to boil. Remove from heat, whisk in the vanilla extract, and pour over the chocolate. Gently begin stirring with a wooden spoon in one direction. Do not forcefully stir. Once the mixture is completely smooth, cover with plastic wrap pressed on the top of the mixture. Let ganache mixture sit at room temperature for 30 minutes, then transfer to the refrigerator for 3–4 hours, or until it reaches scoopable consistency.

3   Line a large baking sheet with parchment paper or a silicone baking mat. Set aside. Remove ganache from the refrigerator. Measure 1 teaspoon, roll between your hands into a ball, and place on the baking sheet. Repeat with rest of ganache. Place the truffles in the refrigerator as you prepare the coating.

4   Make the coating: Melt or temper the bittersweet chocolate (see page 42).

5   Remove truffles from the refrigerator. Working with one truffle at a time, dip completely into the chocolate using a dipping tool (or fork). Place back onto the baking sheet. Repeat with rest of truffles.

6   Melt or temper the white chocolate. With a squeeze bottle (or fork) drizzle over truffles. Press a coffee bean on top of each. Allow the chocolate to completely set at room temperature before serving.

MAKE-AHEAD TIP: See *Ahead of the Game* (page 72).

RED WINE TRUFFLES

Prep time: 1 hour
Total time: 5 hours
Makes: 60 truffles

Ingredients

16oz (454g) semi-sweet chocolate, coarsely chopped

1 cup (240ml) heavy cream

⅓ cup (180ml) red wine (I prefer pinot noir or cabernet sauvignon)

1 tbsp unsalted butter, softened to room temperature and halved

¾ cup (65g) natural unsweetened or Dutch-process cocoa powder

Special Equipment

large baking sheet

With a glass of red wine in one hand and a piece of dark chocolate in the other, all is right in my world. I recently visited a gourmet chocolate shop, and before I knew it, I was ordering a box of their wildly popular pinot noir truffles. I mean, really, can it get any better? The answer is YES—making them at home. You're only four easy steps away from boozy chocolate luxury.

1   Place the semi-sweet chocolate in a large heatproof bowl. Microwave on 50 percent power in four 15-second increments, stirring after each, for a total of 60 seconds. Stir until almost completely melted. Set aside.

2   Pour heavy cream in a small saucepan over medium heat. Whisking occasionally, heat until it just begins to boil. Remove from heat and pour over the chocolate. Gently begin stirring with a wooden spoon in one direction. Do not forcefully stir. Once the chocolate and cream are completely smooth, gently stir in the wine and butter until combined. Cover with plastic wrap pressed on the top of the mixture. Let ganache mixture sit at room temperature for 30 minutes, then transfer to the refrigerator for 3–4 hours, or until it reaches a soft, scoopable consistency.

3   Line a large baking sheet with parchment paper or a silicone baking mat. Set aside. Pour cocoa powder into a bowl.

4   Remove ganache from the refrigerator. Measure 1 teaspoon, roll between your hands into a ball, roll in the cocoa powder, and place on the baking sheet. Repeat with rest of ganache. For pretty presentation, I roll some truffles more heavily in the cocoa than others. Serve immediately or cover tightly and chill in the refrigerator until ready to serve. I like them best served cold.

MAKE-AHEAD TIP: See *Ahead of the Game* (page 72).

CARAMEL FOR DIPPING

Prep time: 30 minutes
Total time: 45 minutes (includes cooling)
Makes: about 2 cups (475ml)

Ingredients

1¾ cups (415ml) heavy cream

2 cups (440g) light brown sugar, packed

¾ cup (180ml) light corn syrup

2 tbsp (¼ stick; 28g) unsalted butter, slightly softened

½ tsp salt

½ tsp vanilla extract

Special Equipment

3-qt (2.8L) heavy-duty saucepan

pastry brush

candy thermometer

This is my prized caramel recipe that I always use for dipping. Its flavor is sweet and concentrated, but not overpowering. I use this specific caramel in several recipes in this cookbook, including Caramel Turtles (page 94), Caramel Apples (page 96), Loaded Caramel Pretzels (page 98), and Twix® Caramel Fudge (page 154). I'm pretty sure caramel goes with just about anything, right?! For a thinner caramel sauce perfect for drizzling, see Easy Caramel Sauce on page 162 (Snickers® Cheesecake).

1   Combine the cream, brown sugar, corn syrup, butter, and salt in a 3-qt (2.8L) heavy-duty saucepan. Using a wooden spoon, stir constantly as the butter melts and the sugar dissolves. The mixture will be thick, cloudy, and dull-looking.

2   Once melted, bring the mixture to a boil without stirring. Once boiling, brush down the sides of the pan with a water-moistened pastry brush. Attach a candy thermometer to the pan, making sure not to let it touch the bottom.

3   Cook the caramel until it reaches 235°F (113°C; soft ball stage). When it hits that temperature, begin stirring lightly once every minute. If any candy splashes up the side of the pan, brush it off with the pastry brush. The caramel will begin to thicken. As soon as the caramel reaches 250°F (121°C; hard ball stage), remove pan from the heat and immediately stir in the vanilla extract.

4   Set the caramel aside to cool for 10–15 minutes and then pour into a glass jar. If not using right away, let cool, uncovered, to room temperature before covering and refrigerating. The caramel will thicken as it cools.

MAKE-AHEAD TIP: Store the caramel in the refrigerator for up to 3 weeks. Warm in the microwave or on the stove before using.

CARAMEL TURTLES

Prep time: 1 hour, 45 minutes (includes cooking the caramel)
Total time: 2 hours, 30 minutes
Makes: 48 turtles

Ingredients

4 cups (396g) pecan halves

2 cups (475ml; the full recipe) Caramel for Dipping (page 92)

8oz (227g) semi-sweet chocolate, coarsely chopped

Special Equipment

2 large baking sheets

double boiler (optional)

These chocolate caramel treats are my mom's absolute favorite dessert on the planet. While I turned up my nose at chocolate turtles when I was younger (pecans? yuck!), I'm all about these caramel-packed treats today. The candies get their cutesy name from their resemblance to the animal. I can eat quite a few of these homemade sweets in one sitting, and when paired with a warm cup of coffee, they're almost impossible to pass up!

1   Line 2 large baking sheets with parchment paper or silicone baking mats. Arrange 48 clusters of 4 pecan halves each with 1 inch (2.5cm) of space between clusters (see photo, below). Set aside.

2   Spoon 2 teaspoons (10ml) of the caramel onto the center of each pecan cluster. Let the caramel cool completely to room temperature, about 30 minutes.

3   Melt or temper the chocolate (see page 42). Spoon 1 teaspoon of chocolate over the caramel on each turtle, then allow chocolate to completely set in the refrigerator for 30 minutes (if chocolate is not tempered) or at room temperature for 45 minutes (if chocolate is tempered).

MAKE-AHEAD TIP: Layer turtles between sheets of parchment or wax paper and store in an airtight container at room temperature in a cool, dry place for up to 2 weeks.

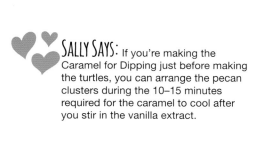

Sally Says: If you're making the Caramel for Dipping just before making the turtles, you can arrange the pecan clusters during the 10–15 minutes required for the caramel to cool after you stir in the vanilla extract.

CARAMEL APPLES

Prep time: 2 hours (includes cooking the caramel)
Total time: 2 hours, 30 minutes
Makes: 8–10 apples

INGREDIENTS

8–10 apples, at room temperature

2 cups (475ml; the full recipe) Caramel for Dipping (page 92)

SPECIAL EQUIPMENT

8–10 lollipop or ice pop sticks

2 large baking sheets

MAKE-AHEAD TIP: Wrap the caramel apples individually in cellophane or plastic wrap and store in the refrigerator for up to 1 week. Remove from the refrigerator about an hour before eating to soften the caramel.

SALLY SAYS: If you're making the Caramel for Dipping right before dipping the apples, allow it to cool for 5–8 minutes after removing from heat and keep the caramel in the pan. If you're warming up already-made Caramel for Dipping, simply warm it on the stove for about 5 minutes, stirring constantly.

Caramel and apples are just made for each other! When I sat down to write this cookbook, I knew I had to include this quintessential fall treat. And what might be even more fun than eating caramel apples is adding festive toppings to them, especially if you have a big group working together. See the suggestions in *To Top It Off* below to get some inspiration, as well as valuable how-to info. For the apples, use your favorite variety. I prefer tart Granny Smith apples, which provide a refreshing contrast to the sweetness of the caramel.

1   Wash the apples with warm water to get rid of any wax coating, then dry thoroughly and remove stems. With light force, insert a lollipop or ice pop stick into the core of each apple. Make sure it is very secure. Set apples aside. Line 2 large baking sheets with parchment paper or silicone baking mats. Set aside.

2   Using the stick to hold the apple and working with one apple at a time, quickly dip each apple halfway into the slightly warm yet thick caramel. Use a spoon to help get the caramel onto the apple, if needed. Allow excess caramel to drip off by holding the apple sideways and spinning it. If you find that the caramel is too thick and has cooled down too much as you are working, warm it back up on the stove for 2–3 minutes, stirring constantly, then continue dipping.

3   Allow caramel (as well as any chocolate and/or other toppings—see *To Top It Off*, below) to set completely on prepared baking sheets, about 30 minutes, before serving.

TO TOP IT OFF

Get creative! Here are some yummy suggestions for enhancing both the look and taste of your caramel apples. If you will not be using melted chocolate, roll the apples in your topping of choice right after completing step 3 in the recipe; after rolling each apple, hold it upright for about 1 minute, then place onto one of the prepared baking sheets. If you will be adding melted chocolate to your apples, let the caramel coating cool completely before dipping in or drizzling with chocolate.

* TURTLE APPLES: Dip one-quarter of the way in 8oz (227g) melted semi-sweet or white chocolate, then roll in 1 cup (109g) finely chopped pecans.

* COOKIES 'N' CREAM APPLES: Dip one-quarter of the way in 8oz (227g) melted white chocolate, then roll in 1 cup (100g) crushed Oreos®.

* RAINBOW APPLES: Roll in 1 cup (160g) rainbow sprinkles.

* BUTTERFINGER® APPLES: Dip one-quarter of the way in 8oz (227g) melted milk chocolate, then roll in 1 cup (125g) crushed Butterfingers®.

* M&M'S® APPLES: Press M&M's® into warm caramel. Use 1–2 cups (208–416g) depending on how many you would like on each apple.

* CHOCOLATE CARAMEL APPLES: Drizzle with 8oz (227g) melted semi-sweet or white chocolate.

LOADED CARAMEL PRETZELS

Prep time: 1 hour, 25 minutes (includes cooking the caramel)
Total time: 2 hours, 25 minutes
Makes: 24–28 pretzel rods

Ingredients

Assorted toppings such as 3 full-size Butterfinger® candy bars, crushed; 1 cup (225g) crushed M&M's®; 1 cup (440g) finely chopped pecans

2 cups (475ml; the full recipe) Caramel for Dipping (page 92)

24–28 pretzel rods

Special Equipment

2 large baking sheets

There is nothing like a sweet treat with a satisfying crunch and salty bite. This loaded recipe begins with pretzel rods that are then coated in caramel and finished off with toppings, such as crushed Butterfinger® candy bars, crushed M&M's®, or even chopped pecans and chocolate for a fun spin on turtles (see step 4, below). I created this recipe with kids in mind—they will have a ball helping you decorate the pretzels with toppings. Serving suggestion: place a bunch of the finished pretzels in a few tall glasses, caramel side up, and let guests choose which topping is their dessert destiny. (I'm quite passionate about Loaded Caramel Pretzels.)

1   Place toppings in separate medium-size bowls or on medium-size plates. Set aside. Line 2 large baking sheets with parchment paper or silicone baking mats. Set aside.

2   Working with one pretzel at a time, quickly dip each pretzel halfway into the slightly warm yet thick caramel. Allow excess to drip off by very gently tapping the pretzel on the side of the measuring glass, making sure not to break the pretzel. If the caramel is too thin, allow it to sit a little longer at room temperature to thicken so that it will stick to the pretzel.

3   Once the pretzel is halfway coated with caramel, roll the caramel portion of the pretzel in a topping until all sides are coated. Place pretzel on the prepared baking sheet to allow caramel to set. Repeat with each pretzel. If you find that the caramel is falling off the sides of the finished pretzels as you are working, simply turn/rotate them to make sure the caramel stays put as it sets. I use about 1½ tablespoons (22ml) of caramel per pretzel, though this amount can vary slightly.

4   Optional: If making "turtle pretzels" as described in the recipe intro, melt 4 ounces (113g) of chocolate using my instructions on page 44; roll caramel-coated pretzels into the pecan pieces and then drizzle with melted chocolate.

5   Allow caramel and chocolate to completely set, about 1 hour.

Sally Says: If you're making the Caramel for Dipping right before dipping the pretzels, allow it to cool for 10 minutes after removing from heat, then pour into a 2-cup (475ml) measuring glass for easy dipping. If you're warming up already-made Caramel for Dipping, simply warm it on the stove for about 5 minutes, stirring constantly.

Sally Also Says: To crush candy bars or even chop the nuts, simply pulse in a food processor or blender until crushed. Alternatively, you can place in a large zipped-top bag and roll with a rolling pin until crushed.

MAKE-AHEAD TIP: Store pretzels lined between sheets of parchment or wax paper in an airtight container in the refrigerator or at room temperature in a cool, dry place for up to 1 week.

CHEWY CREAM CARAMELS

Prep time: 35 minutes
Total time: 4 hours, 35 minutes
Makes: 64 x 1-in (2.5cm) squares or 32 1 x 2-in (2.5 x 5cm) rectangles

INGREDIENTS

1½ cups (355ml) heavy cream

1 cup (200g) sugar

½ cup (100g) light brown sugar

⅓ cup (80ml) light corn syrup

1 tsp vanilla extract

1 tsp salt

1 tbsp (⅛ stick; 14g) unsalted butter, softened to room temperature, plus more if using for greasing

SPECIAL EQUIPMENT

8-in (20cm) square baking pan

3-qt (2.8L) heavy-duty saucepan

pastry brush

candy thermometer

For this recipe, I use a variation of Caramel for Dipping (page 92). While both caramels are cooked to the same temperature, I use less brown sugar and cream (both of which contain a lot of moisture) in this recipe to produce a firmer caramel that will hold its shape when cut. These incredibly chewy, creamy caramels make the perfect homemade gift. For the ultimate caramel experience, I suggest placing a piece . . . or two . . . in your mouth and letting it melt on your tongue before chewing. Talk about dreamy!

1   Line an 8-in (20cm) square baking pan with aluminum foil, leaving enough overhang on the sides to easily remove the caramel once it has set. Lightly butter or spray with nonstick cooking spray. Set aside.

2   Combine the cream, sugar, brown sugar, and corn syrup in a 3-qt (2.8L) heavy-duty saucepan. Using a wooden spoon, stir constantly as the sugars dissolve. The mixture will be thick, cloudy, and dull-looking. Once the sugars have dissolved, turn the burner up to medium-high heat and bring the mixture to a boil without stirring. Once boiling, brush down the sides of the pan with a water-moistened pastry brush. Attach a candy thermometer to the pan, making sure not to let it touch the bottom.

3   As the mixture boils, gently stir every 2 minutes. If any candy splashes up the sides of the pan, brush it off with the pastry brush. After you stir, do not be alarmed if the temperature temporarily drops. Once at 250°F (121°C; hard ball stage), remove the pan from heat. Quickly stir in the vanilla, salt, and butter until combined. Pour the hot caramel into the prepared baking pan and allow to cool at room temperature, uncovered, for 4 hours, or until set. I prefer letting it set overnight.

4   Once set, remove the caramel from the pan by lifting out the aluminum foil, invert onto a cutting board, peel away foil, and turn back over. Using a sharp knife, cut into squares or rectangles.

MAKE-AHEAD TIP: I suggest wrapping the caramels in wax paper or cellophane, which makes them wonderful for gift-giving and extends their shelf life. Wrapped caramels can be stored at room temperature in a cool, dry place or in the refrigerator for up to 3 weeks. Unwrapped caramels can be stored layered between sheets of parchment or wax paper for up to 2 weeks.

CHOCOLATE SEA-SALT CARAMELS

Prep time: 1 hour
Total time: 6 hours
Makes: 64 x 1-in (2.5cm) squares or 32 1 x 2-in (2.5 x 5cm) rectangles

INGREDIENTS

1 batch Chewy Cream Caramels (page 100)

6 or 10oz (170 or 283g) semi-sweet chocolate, coarsely chopped

sea salt

SPECIAL EQUIPMENT

2 large baking sheets

double boiler (optional)

dipping tool (optional)

For when you want a truly decadent caramel treat, this recipe takes my Chewy Cream Caramels (page 100) to the next level by dipping them in chocolate and sprinkling them with sea salt. You're welcome!

1 Line 2 large baking sheets with parchment paper or silicone baking mats. Set aside.

2 Melt or temper the chocolate (see page 42), using 6 ounces (170g) if only coating the caramels halfway and using 10 ounces (283g) if fully coating.

3 Dip the Chewy Creamy Caramels one by one into the chocolate, either halfway or in full. If coating halfway, you can use your fingers to hold onto one side of the caramel as you dip the other side into the chocolate. If fully coating, use a dipping tool (or fork). After dipping, place the caramel onto one of the lined baking sheets. Sprinkle with sea salt and repeat with rest of caramels.

4 Allow the chocolate to completely set at room temperature for 1 hour before serving.

MAKE-AHEAD TIP: If chocolate has not been tempered, follow the make-ahead instructions for Chewy Cream Caramels on page 100. If chocolate has been tempered, layer unwrapped caramels between sheets of parchment or wax paper and store in an airtight container at room temperature in a cool, dry place for up to 2 weeks. Store wrapped caramels up to 3 weeks.

OVERLOADED CINNAMON SPICE BRITTLE

Prep time: 30 minutes
Total time: 1 hour
Makes: 2 pounds (907g)

INGREDIENTS

2 cups (400g) sugar

½ tsp salt

1 cup (240ml) light corn syrup

½ cup (120ml) water, room temperature

¼ cup (½ stick; 57g) unsalted butter, slightly softened and quartered, plus more if using for greasing

1½ tsp baking soda

1 tsp vanilla

1 tsp ground cinnamon

1 cup (143g) raw almonds

1 cup (130g) raw cashews

¾ cup (90g) dried cranberries

¾ cup (98g) raw pumpkin seeds (a.k.a. pepitas)

SPECIAL EQUIPMENT

12 x 17-in (30 x 43cm) jelly roll pan or a similar-sized rimmed baking sheet

silicone baking mat (recommended

3-qt (2.8L) heavy-duty saucepan

pastry brush

candy thermometer

I have to be honest with you . . . this brittle exceeded my expectations and then some! I wanted to create a fun twist on Peanut Brittle (page 112) for this book, and a slew of nuts came to mind. To make it even jazzier, I threw in some dried cranberries and cinnamon. Each crunchy, buttery bite reminds me of cool fall days. I normally have a ton of self-control around desserts (well, except around page 142), but I could NOT stop grabbing piece after piece of this overloaded brittle. Just could NOT. All caps. I urge you to measure and set out the butter, baking soda, vanilla, cinnamon, nuts, cranberries, and seeds before you start making the recipe.

1 Line a 12 x 17-in (30 x 43cm) jelly roll pan with a silicone baking mat. Alternatively, lightly butter or spray with nonstick cooking spray. I do not suggest parchment paper or aluminum foil. Set aside.

2 Combine the sugar, salt, corn syrup, and water in a 3-qt (2.8L) heavy-duty saucepan over medium heat. Stir constantly with a wooden spoon until the sugar is dissolved, then brush down the sides of the pan with a water-moistened pastry brush to prevent the candy from burning there. (Alternatively, you can lightly butter the inside edges of the saucepan with butter before beginning this recipe.) Attach a candy thermometer to the pan, making sure not to let it touch the bottom.

3 Bring candy to a boil, stirring occasionally. Once boiling, stop stirring. As the sugar cooks, the candy will go from clear on top to frothy bubbles on top. To avoid scorching, begin lightly stirring the candy occasionally once it reaches 265°F (129°C; hard ball stage). Cook the candy until it reaches 300°F (149°C; hard crack stage).

4 Working quickly and carefully (it's hot!), remove candy from the heat and stir in the butter, baking soda, vanilla, cinnamon, nuts, cranberries, and pumpkin seeds until combined. The candy will immediately foam and bubble. Pour out onto prepared jelly roll pan and, using 2 forks, pull the candy into a large rectangle so the add-ins are in 1 even layer. Allow to cool completely at room temperature, about 30 minutes. Snap brittle into pieces.

MAKE-AHEAD TIP: Store brittle in an airtight container at room temperature for up to 2 weeks. Brittle freezes well. Break it up as directed, place into an airtight container, and freeze up to 3 months.

SALLY SAYS: If using salted nuts, omit salt in recipe.

NUTS AND SWEET TREATS

If the thought of a candy thermometer still frightens you, don't fret. You won't need it for the recipes in this chapter! The next several pages are full of easy recipes, such as candied nuts, two-ingredient peanut clusters, and puppy chow (not the dog food—don't worry).

The first half of this chapter is a little nut-heavy. I know many people cringe at the addition of nuts in brownies, cookies, and other desserts, but I love it. What's funny is that I despised nuts when I was little, often picking out nuts from my mom's oatmeal raisin walnut cookies. I also hated Brussels sprouts, but I've learned to love 'em. Not as much as nuts.

If nuts aren't your thing or if you have an allergy, all is not lost. Skip to the second half of this chapter where you'll find two variations of caramel corn (you can leave the nuts out of this one!) and a cereal bar treat that is as gooey as it is colorful. How sweet it is!

CANDIED NUTS

Prep time: 15 minutes
Total time: 1 hour, 30 minutes
Makes: 6 cups (638g)

Ingredients

5 cups (495g) pecan halves, unsalted

1 cup (143g) whole almonds, unsalted

2 large egg whites

2 tbsp water

2 cups (400g) sugar

2½ tsp ground cinnamon

2 tsp salt

Special Equipment

2 large baking sheets

handheld or stand mixer fitted with a whisk attachment

Nuts, often praised for their healthy fats and wholesome goodness, get completely stripped of their innocent reputation here. This devilishly salty-sweet candied-nuts recipe comes from my mom's dear friend Sharyn. I can't remember a single Christmas without a bowl of these crunchy-coated nuts. Her recipe calls for only pecans, but I've added some almonds for varying texture and appearance. This treat is easy to make and even easier to polish off completely. I'm not kidding; you'll find yourself with an empty bowl in minutes. Oops.

1   Preheat oven to 300°F (149°C). Line 2 large baking sheets with parchment paper or use silicone baking mats. Set aside.

2   Mix pecans and almonds in a large bowl. Set aside. With a handheld or stand mixer fitted with a whisk attachment, beat the egg whites with the water on high speed in a medium bowl until stiff peaks form, about 4 minutes (see photo, below). With a rubber spatula, gently fold in the sugar, cinnamon, and salt until combined.

3   Pour/spoon sugar mixture over nuts and stir to coat completely. Spread nuts over the prepared baking sheets and bake for 45 minutes, stirring every 15 minutes. Allow to cool completely before serving.

MAKE-AHEAD TIP: Store nuts in an airtight container at room temperature in a cool, dry place for up to 1 month. For longer storage, freeze up to 2 months; thaw overnight in the refrigerator before serving.

SEA-SALT MAPLE CINNAMON ALMONDS

Prep time: 20 minutes
Total time: 1 hour, 5 minutes
Makes: 2 cups (286g)

Ingredients

2 cups (286g) unsalted almonds

¼ cup (60ml) pure maple syrup

1½ tsp ground cinnamon

¼ tsp sea salt

Special Equipment

large baking sheet

MAKE-AHEAD TIP: Store nuts in an airtight container at room temperature in a cool, dry place for up to 1 month. For longer storage, freeze up to 2 months; thaw overnight in the refrigerator before serving.

The day I made these salty-sweet cinnamon-spiced almonds was the day my life changed forever. A little dramatic? Ok, maybe. These little almonds may look innocent, but they pack enough mouthwatering flavor to put all other nuts to shame. These delicious almonds compete with Candied Nuts (page 120) for my favorite Christmas snack. Please, guys, don't make me choose!

1   Preheat oven to 300°F (150°C). Line a large baking sheet with parchment paper or a silicone baking mat. Spread almonds on top and toast for 8–10 minutes. Remove almonds from the oven, keeping the oven on, and allow almonds to cool for 5 minutes before handling.

2   In a large bowl, combine the toasted almonds, maple syrup, and cinnamon. Stir to combine; make sure each almond is coated well. Spread the coated almonds back onto the baking sheet and sprinkle with sea salt. Bake for 24–25 minutes, stirring every 8 minutes.

3   Remove almonds from the oven and allow to cool completely on the baking sheet before serving.

COCOA ROASTED ALMONDS

Prep time: 5 minutes
Total time: 45 minutes
Makes: 1 cup (143g)

Ingredients

- 1 cup (143g) unsalted almonds
- 1 tbsp pure maple syrup
- 2 tbsp unsweetened cocoa powder
- 1 tbsp all-purpose flour

Special Equipment

- large baking sheet

MAKE-AHEAD TIP: Store nuts in an airtight container at room temperature in a cool, dry place for up to 1 month. For longer storage, freeze up to 2 months; thaw overnight in the refrigerator before serving.

My friend Kristen and I love cocoa almonds. We used to get our fix with a store-bought version, but that was before I taught myself how to make these slightly sweet almonds from scratch. They are so easy! If you're looking for a simple way to kick your almonds up a notch, add cocoa and roast 'em.

1. Preheat oven to 300°F (150°C). Line a large baking sheet with parchment paper or a silicone baking mat. Set aside.

2. Combine the almonds and maple syrup in a medium-size bowl. Stir with a rubber spatula to coat all of the almonds evenly. Stir in the cocoa powder and flour, making sure each almond is well coated with the mixture. Spread the coated almonds onto the baking sheet and bake for 20 minutes, tossing once at the 10-minute mark.

3. Remove almonds from the oven and allow to cool completely on the baking sheet before serving.

ROCKY ROAD FUDGE

Prep time: 45 minutes
Total time: 3 hours, 45 minutes
Makes: 64 x 1-in (2.5cm) squares

INGREDIENTS

2½ tbsp unsalted butter, softened to room temperature, divided

2 cups (400g) sugar

1 cup (240ml) heavy cream

¼ cup (60ml) light corn syrup

¼ tsp salt

6oz (170g) semi-sweet chocolate, coarsely chopped

1 tsp vanilla extract

1 cup (145g) salted peanuts

1½ cups (75g) miniature marshmallows

SPECIAL EQUIPMENT

8-in (20cm) square baking pan

3-qt (2.8L) heavy-duty saucepan

pastry brush

candy thermometer

handheld or stand mixer fitted with a paddle attachment

How do you turn a truly magnificent chocolate fudge into something even more divine? A few salty peanuts here, a lot of dreamy marshmallows there. This Rocky Road Fudge is for those of us who crave texture. And it delivers! Though the nuts and marshmallows add a whole new layer of awesome, the chocolate is still the star of the show.

1   Line an 8-in (20cm) square baking pan with aluminum foil, leaving enough overhang on the sides to easily remove the fudge once it has set. Lightly grease the foil with ½ tablespoon butter. Set pan and remaining butter aside.

2   Combine the sugar, cream, corn syrup, and salt in a 3-qt (2.8L) heavy-duty saucepan over medium heat. Using a wooden spoon, stir constantly as the sugar dissolves. Once dissolved, bring the mixture to a boil without stirring. Once boiling, brush down the sides of the pan with a water-moistened pastry brush.

3   Temporarily remove pan from the heat and stir in the chocolate until combined and smooth. Return to heat and attach a candy thermometer to the pan, making sure not to let it touch the bottom.

4   Without stirring, cook the mixture until the thermometer registers 234°F (112°C; soft ball stage), about 10–15 minutes. Turn off the stove and remove pan from the heat. Without mixing in, simply add the 2 remaining tablespoons (28g) of butter. Place the pan in shallow ice water to help the mixture quickly cool down to 110°F (43°C).

5   Once at 110°F (43°C), gently mix in the butter (which will have now melted on top by now) with a wooden spoon. Without scraping the sides of the pan (this causes graininess in the fudge), spoon the mixture into the bowl of your stand mixer or, if using a handheld mixer, into a large mixing bowl. Add the vanilla and beat on medium-high for 10 minutes, until the mixture thickens and loses its shine.

6   By hand, fold in the peanuts and marshmallows until just combined. The mixture will be extremely thick. Spread the fudge into the prepared 8-in (20cm) square baking pan and use a rubber spatula or wooden spoon to smooth it into an even layer.

7   Cover with aluminum foil and allow to set at room temperature for at least 4 hours. Once set, remove the fudge from the pan by lifting out the aluminum foil. Invert the fudge onto a cutting board, peel away foil, and turn the fudge back over. Using a large sharp knife, slice the fudge into 1-in (2.5cm) squares.

MAKE-AHEAD TIP: See *Be Prepared* (page 137).

PEANUT BUTTER FUDGE

Prep time: 25 minutes
Total time: 3 hours, 25 minutes or overnight
Makes: 64 x 1-in (2.5cm) squares

Ingredients

1¾ cups (350g) sugar

¾ cup (180ml) heavy cream

¾ cup (185g) creamy peanut butter

¼ tsp salt

1 tsp vanilla extract

2oz (57g) semi-sweet chocolate, coarsely chopped

Special Equipment

8-in (20cm) square baking pan

3-qt (2.8L) heavy-duty saucepan

pastry brush

candy thermometer

Moderation? Self-control? What is that nonsense?! All hail the old-fashioned, sweet, and simple peanut butter fudge, ruining one diet at a time. And because I'm completely ridiculous, I like to swirl chocolate into my peanut butter fudge.

1   Line an 8-in (20cm) square baking pan with aluminum foil, leaving enough overhang on the sides to easily remove the fudge once it has set. Set aside.

2   Combine sugar and cream in a 3-qt (2.8L) heavy-duty saucepan over medium heat. Attach a candy thermometer to the side of the pan, making sure not to let it touch the bottom. Stirring lightly every 5 minutes with a wooden spoon, bring the mixture to a boil. Once boiling, stop stirring and allow the mixture to continue to boil until the thermometer registers 250°F (121°C; hard ball stage). Remove pan from the heat and stir in the peanut butter, salt, and vanilla.

3   Gently fold in the chocolate, creating swirls. Do not stir to completely combine; you want those pretty chocolate swirls. Pour mixture into the prepared baking pan. Do not scrape the sides of the saucepan. Smooth fudge into an even layer.

4   Cover with aluminum foil and refrigerate for 3 hours, or until set. Alternatively, you can let the covered fudge set at room temperature overnight. Once set, remove the fudge from the pan by lifting out the aluminum foil. Invert the fudge onto a cutting board, peel away foil, and turn the fudge back over. Using a large sharp knife, slice the fudge into 1-in (2.5cm) squares.

MAKE-AHEAD TIP: See *Be Prepared* (page 137).

FLUFFERNUTTER SWIRL FUDGE

Prep time: 25 minutes
Total time: 3 hours, 25 minutes or overnight
Makes: 64 x 1-in (2.5cm) squares

INGREDIENTS

1¾ cups (350g) sugar

¾ cup (180ml) heavy cream

¾ cup (185g) creamy peanut butter

¼ tsp salt

1 tsp vanilla extract

2oz (57g) semi-sweet chocolate, coarsely chopped

1 cup (50g) miniature marshmallows

SPECIAL EQUIPMENT

8-in (20cm) square baking pan

3-qt (2.8L) heavy-duty saucepan

pastry brush

candy thermometer

Do you know what a fluffernutter is? It's the whimsically named sandwich that combines creamy peanut butter and sweet marshmallow crème between two pieces of white bread. As healthy as a turkey on wheat? We can pretend. This fudge is inspired by the MANY memories I have of eating fluffernutters with my sister, Sarah. The fudge begins the same way as Peanut Butter Fudge (page 142). This one's for you, Sare!

1   Line an 8-in (20cm) square baking pan with aluminum foil, leaving enough overhang on the sides to easily remove the fudge once it has set. Set aside.

2   Combine sugar and cream in a 3-qt (2.8L) heavy-duty saucepan over medium heat. Attach a candy thermometer to the side of the pan, making sure not to let it touch the bottom. Stirring lightly every 5 minutes with a wooden spoon, bring the mixture to a boil. Once boiling, stop stirring and allow the mixture to continue to boil until the thermometer registers 250°F (121°C; hard ball stage). Remove pan from the heat and stir in the peanut butter, salt, and vanilla.

3   Let the fudge rest for 10 minutes to slightly cool, then gently fold in the marshmallows. The marshmallows will begin to melt and create swirls as you stir. Do not stir to completely combine; you want those pretty swirls. Pour into the prepared pan and smooth into an even layer.

4   Cover with aluminum foil and refrigerate for 3 hours, or until set. Alternatively, you can let the covered fudge set at room temperature overnight. Once set, remove the fudge from the pan by lifting out the aluminum foil. Invert the fudge onto a cutting board, peel away foil, and turn the fudge back over. Using a large sharp knife, slice the fudge into 1-in (2.5cm) squares.

MAKE-AHEAD TIP: See *Be Prepared* (page 137).

MAPLE WALNUT FUDGE

Prep time: 45 minutes
Total time: 4 hours, 45 minutes
Makes: 64 x 1-in (2.5cm) squares

Ingredients

2½ tbsp unsalted butter, softened to room temperature, divided

¾ cup (180ml) pure maple syrup

1½ cups (355ml) heavy cream

3 cups (600g) sugar

3 tbsp light corn syrup

¼ tsp salt

2 tsp vanilla extract

1½ cups (175g) chopped raw unsalted walnuts

Special Equipment

8-in (20cm) square baking pan

3-qt (2.8L) heavy-duty saucepan

pastry brush

candy thermometer

handheld or stand mixer fitted with a paddle attachment

Am I allowed to choose favorites? I'm a huge maple lover, so this fudge has always been my first-choice flavor. Rich and buttery, this from-scratch fudge takes the cake for comfort food. It reminds me of summer days walking on the boardwalk, passing by fudge kitchens, and grabbing two, five, ten free samples. The addition of walnuts gives the perfect contrast in texture to the smooth yet slightly crumbly fudge. Make sure you use pure maple syrup—not breakfast syrup, sugar-free, or imitation. Chopped pecans make a lovely substitute for the walnuts.

1   Line an 8-in (20cm) square baking pan with aluminum foil, leaving enough overhang on the sides to easily remove the fudge once it has set. Lightly grease the foil with ½ tablespoon butter. Set pan and remaining butter aside.

2   Combine maple syrup, heavy cream, sugar, corn syrup, and salt in a 3-qt (2.8L) heavy-duty saucepan over medium heat. Using a wooden spoon, stir constantly as the sugar dissolves. Once dissolved, bring the mixture to a boil without stirring. Once boiling, brush down the sides of the pan with a water-moistened pastry brush. Attach a candy thermometer to the pan, making sure not to let it touch the bottom.

3   Without stirring, cook the mixture until the thermometer registers 238°F (114°C; soft ball stage). Remove pan from the heat. Without mixing in, simply add the remaining 2 tablespoons butter. Place the pan in shallow ice water to help the mixture quickly cool down to 110°F (43°C).

4   Once at 110°F (43°C), gently mix in the butter (which will have melted on top by now) with a wooden spoon. Without scraping the sides of the pan (this causes graininess in the fudge), spoon the mixture into the bowl of your stand mixer or, if using a handheld mixer, into a large mixing bowl. Add the vanilla and beat on medium-high for 10 minutes until the mixture thickens and loses its shine. Beat in the walnuts on low speed until combined, about 1 minute. Pour the fudge into the prepared baking pan and use a rubber spatula or wooden spoon to smooth it into an even layer.

5   Cover with aluminum foil and allow to start setting at room temperature for 1 hour before transferring to the refrigerator to fully set for another 4–5 hours. Once set, remove the fudge from the pan by lifting out the aluminum foil. Invert the fudge onto a cutting board, peel away foil, and turn the fudge back over. Using a large sharp knife, slice the fudge into 1-in (2.5cm) squares.

MAKE-AHEAD TIP: This fudge is best stored in the refrigerator. Layer cooled fudge pieces between sheets of parchment or wax paper and store in an airtight container in the refrigerator for up to 3 weeks. For freezing instructions, see *Be Prepared* (page 137).

YORK® PEPPERMINT PATTIE CUPCAKES

Prep time: 25 minutes
Total time: 1 hour, 45 minutes (includes cooling)
Makes: 12 cupcakes

Cupcakes

½ cup (43g) unsweetened natural cocoa powder

¾ cup (95g) all-purpose flour

¾ tsp baking powder

½ tsp baking soda

¼ tsp salt

2 large eggs, room temperature

½ cup (100g) sugar

½ cup (110g) light brown sugar, packed

⅓ cup (80ml) vegetable oil

2 tsp vanilla extract

½ cup (120ml) buttermilk

Peppermint Vanilla Frosting

1 cup (2 sticks; 227g) unsalted butter, softened to room temperature

4½ cups (540g) confectioners' sugar, plus ½ cup (60g) if needed

¼ cup (60ml) heavy cream, plus 1 tbsp if needed

1 tsp vanilla extract

¼ tsp peppermint extract, plus more if needed

⅛ tsp salt, plus pinch if needed

6 snack size York® Peppermint Patties, sliced in half

Special Equipment

12-count muffin pan

12 cupcake liners

handheld or stand mixer fitted with a paddle or whisk attachment

piping bag and Wilton® 1M tip (both optional; using a knife to frost is okay)

I went through a serious York® Peppermint Pattie obsession in high school, when you could find dozens of crumpled-up wrappers inside my locker. My love for the candy bar hasn't subsided since. That's why I make these rich chocolate cupcakes with a peppermint frosting. And, of course, that familiar candy topper. Be careful with the peppermint extract in the frosting—a little goes a long way!

1 Preheat the oven to 350°F (180°C). Line a 12-cup muffin pan with cupcake liners. Set aside.

2 Make the cupcakes: Whisk the cocoa powder, flour, baking powder, baking soda, and salt together in a large bowl until combined. Set aside. In a medium bowl, whisk the eggs, sugar, brown sugar, oil, and vanilla together until completely smooth. Pour half of the wet ingredients into the dry ingredients. Then add half of the buttermilk. Gently whisk—about 5 stirs. Repeat with the remaining wet ingredients and buttermilk. Whisk until just combined; do not overmix. The batter will be a little thin.

3 Pour or spoon batter into cupcake liners, filling halfway. Bake for 18–21 minutes, or until the tops of the cupcakes spring back when gently touched and a toothpick inserted into the center comes out clean. Do not overbake; your cupcakes will quickly dry out. Allow to cool in the pan for 5 minutes, then transfer to a rack to cool completely.

4 Make the frosting: With a handheld or stand mixer fitted with a paddle or whisk attachment, beat the butter on medium speed in a large bowl until creamy, about 2 minutes. Add 4½ cups (540g) confectioners' sugar, ¼ cup (60ml) cream, vanilla and peppermint extracts, and salt with the mixer running on low. Increase the mixer to high speed and beat for 3 full minutes. Add ½ cup (60g) confectioners' sugar if the frosting is too thin or add 1 tablespoon of cream if frosting is too thick. Taste the frosting; add an extra drop of peppermint extract for more peppermint flavor if desired and/or an extra pinch of salt if frosting is too sweet. Frost cooled cupcakes and stick a Peppermint Pattie half on each. Leftover prepared cupcakes can be stored covered tightly at room temperature for up to 3 days.

MAKE-AHEAD TIP: If you wish to prepare a day in advance, keep cupcakes covered tightly at room temperature and refrigerate frosting in an airtight container. Bring frosting to room temperature before spreading on cupcakes. Unfrosted cupcakes can be frozen up to 2 months; thaw overnight in the refrigerator and bring to room temperature before frosting and serving.

THE GREAT MILKY WAY® CAKE

Prep time: 1 hour
Total time: 4 hours, 30 minutes
Makes: 10 servings

Cake

2 cups (230g) cake flour

1¾ tsp baking powder

½ tsp salt

3 large eggs, room temperature and separated

½ cup (1 stick; 114g) unsalted butter, softened to room temperature

1½ cups (300g) sugar

1 tbsp vanilla extract

⅔ cup (160ml) whole milk, room temperature

Easy Caramel Sauce

1 cup (220g) light brown sugar, packed

½ cup (120ml) heavy cream

4 tbsp (½ stick; 57g) unsalted butter, quartered

¼ tsp salt

1 tsp vanilla extract

Frosting

1¼ cups (2½ sticks; 284g) unsalted butter, softened to room temperature

3½ cups (420g) confectioners' sugar, plus 2 tbsp if needed

¾ cup (65g) natural unsweetened or Dutch-process cocoa powder

¼ tsp salt, plus pinch if needed

1 tsp vanilla extract

¼ cup (60ml) heavy cream, plus 1 tbsp if needed

1 cup (160g) chopped Milky Way® bars, divided (about 10 fun-size bars)

Special Equipment

2 x 9-in (23cm) cake pans

flour sifter

handheld or stand mixer fitted with a paddle and whisk attachment

I've made a ton of cakes from scratch, but nothing compares to the greatness of this candy bar–filled beauty. It's a cross between vanilla cake and buttery moist yellow cake. Cake flour produces a blissfully soft cake, as you'll notice with the first bite. The cake itself is to die for, but the milk chocolate frosting, layer of Milky Ways®, and caramel drizzle completely transform it into something extraordinary. The layers can rise up quite tall, so make sure you level them off as needed (see page 164 for instructions).

SALLY SAYS: The reason for separating the eggs is to create an ultra-fluffy cake crumb. Egg yolks are mixed in with the wet ingredients, and voluminous whipped egg whites are folded into the batter before it goes into the oven. Whip the egg whites only until soft peaks form—right when the peaks are just starting to hold.

1 Preheat oven to 350°F (180°C). Spray two 9-in (23cm) cake pans with nonstick cooking spray. Set aside.

2 Make the cake: Sift the cake flour, baking powder, and salt together in a large bowl. Set aside.

3 With a handheld or stand mixer fitted with a whisk attachment, beat the egg whites on high speed in a medium bowl until soft peaks form, about 2–3 minutes. Set aside.

4 With a handheld or stand mixer fitted with a paddle attachment, beat the butter on high speed in a large bowl until smooth and creamy, about 1 minute. Add the sugar and beat on high speed for 3–4 minutes until creamed. Scrape down the sides and up the bottom of the bowl with a rubber spatula as needed. Add the egg yolks and vanilla extract. Beat on medium-high speed until

continued on page 164

combined. Scrape the bowl again as needed. With the mixer on low speed, add the dry ingredients in 3 additions, alternating with the milk and mixing each addition just until incorporated. Do not overmix. Using a rubber spatula, gently fold in the egg whites until combined. The batter will be slightly thick.

5   Pour or spoon the batter evenly into prepared cake pans. Bake for 25–28 minutes, or until a toothpick inserted into the center of one cake comes out clean. During bake time, loosely cover the cakes with aluminum foil if you find the tops are browning too quickly. Remove cakes from the oven and allow to cool completely in the pans set on a wire rack.

6   Make the caramel sauce: As the cakes cool, combine the brown sugar, heavy cream, butter, and salt in a medium-size saucepan over medium heat. Stir constantly with a wooden spoon until butter is melted, about 2–3 minutes. Bring to a boil and, without stirring, allow to boil for 3 minutes. Remove saucepan from the heat and stir in the vanilla extract. Allow to cool for 15 minutes, then pour into a glass jar and cover tightly. Allow to cool at room temperature, about 45 minutes, or in the refrigerator, about 30 minutes, before using on the cake.

7   Make the frosting: After the cakes and caramel have cooled, using a handheld or stand mixer fitted with a paddle or whisk attachment, beat the butter on medium speed in a large bowl until creamy, about 2 minutes. Add 3½ cups (420g) confectioners' sugar, cocoa powder, salt, vanilla, and ¼ cup (60ml) cream with the mixer running on low. Once added, increase the mixer to high speed and beat for 3 full minutes. Add 2 tablespoons of confectioners' sugar if the frosting is too thin or add 1 tablespoon of cream if the frosting is too thick. Taste the frosting; add an extra pinch of salt if frosting is too sweet. Measure 1 cup (328g) of frosting and place it in a separate bowl. Fold in ½ cup (80g) of the chopped candy bars into the 1 cup (328g) of frosting. Set aside.

8   Frost and assemble the cake: Level the cake layers to create a flat surface (see "How to Level a Cake," left). Place 1 cake layer on a cake stand or large serving plate. Evenly spread the frosting–candy bar mixture on top. Be gentle, as the cake is fragile and the frosting is thick and chunky. Top with second cake and spread the plain frosting all over the top and sides. Decorate the top with remaining chopped candy bars. Serve with caramel sauce drizzled on top. Cover any leftover cake tightly and store at room temperature for up to 3 days or in the refrigerator for up to 5 days.

········ HOW TO LEVEL A CAKE ········

✳ Place a layer on a large cutting board. Using a serrated knife, carefully move the knife back and forth across the top of the cake in a sawing motion to remove the crown. Try to keep the knife level as you do this. Repeat with the second layer.

✳ Another option is to use a cake leveler.

✳ Instead of discarding the crowns, crumble them over ice cream.

✳ Alternatively, you can crumble them up and use them to decorate the sides of the frosted cake.

MAKE-AHEAD TIP: To prepare a day in advance, keep cakes covered tightly at room temperature and refrigerate prepared frosting in an airtight container. Bring frosting to room temperature before spreading on the cake. Frosted cake can be frozen up to 2 months; when ready to serve, thaw overnight in the refrigerator and bring to room temperature before serving. Unfrosted cake layers can also be frozen up to 2 months; thaw overnight in the refrigerator and bring to room temperature before frosting, assembling, and serving. As everything is coming to room temperature, make the caramel sauce in step 6.

TOFFEE LOVER'S CUPCAKES

Prep time: 50 minutes
Total time: 2 hours, 10 minutes
Makes: 18 cupcakes

The only thing better than a cupcake with chocolate frosting is a cupcake with two chocolate frostings and plenty of chopped Heath® bars. Just sayin'.

Cupcakes

Cake batter for The Great Milky Way® Cake (page 162)

Chocolate Topping

½ cup (1 stick; 114g) unsalted butter

1 cup plus 2 tbsp (204g) milk chocolate chips

1½ cups (215g) chopped Heath® bars

Milk Chocolate Frosting

1 cup (2 sticks; 227g) unsalted butter, softened to room temperature

3½ cups (420g) confectioners' sugar, plus 2 tbsp if needed

½ cup (43g) unsweetened cocoa powder

½ tsp salt, plus pinch if needed

2 tsp vanilla extract

3 tbsp heavy cream or milk, plus 1 tbsp if needed

Special Equipment

12-count muffin pan

12 cupcake liners

flour sifter

handheld or stand mixer fitted with a paddle attachment

piping bag and Wilton® 1M tip (both optional; using a knife to frost is okay)

1 Preheat oven to 350°F (180°C). Line a 12-count muffin pan with cupcake liners. This recipe makes 18 cupcakes, so you will have 6 cupcakes to bake in a second batch.

2 Make the cupcakes: Prepare the batter by following steps 2, 3, and 4 on pages 162–164.

3 Spoon batter into cupcake liners, filling halfway. Bake for 22–24 minutes, or until the tops of the cupcakes spring back when gently touched and a toothpick inserted into the center comes out clean. Allow to cool in the pan for 5 minutes, then transfer to a rack to cool completely.

4 Make the chocolate topping: Melt the butter and chocolate chips in a small saucepan over medium heat, stirring constantly, about 5 minutes. Once melted and smooth, remove pan from the heat. Allow to cool and slightly thicken for 5 minutes, then pour into a wide, shallow bowl. Pour the chopped Heath® bars into a separate wide, shallow bowl. Dip the top of each cooled cupcake into the chocolate mixture, then roll the top edges in the Heath® bars. Set cupcakes aside for 20 minutes to allow the chocolate topping to set.

5 Make the frosting: With a handheld or stand mixer fitted with a paddle or whisk attachment, beat the butter on medium speed in a large bowl until creamy, about 2 minutes. Add 3½ cups confectioners' sugar, cocoa powder, salt, vanilla, and 3 tbsp cream with the mixer running on low. Increase to high speed and beat for 3 full minutes. Add 2 tablespoons of confectioners' sugar if the frosting is too thin or add 1 tablespoon of cream if the frosting is too thick. Taste the frosting; add an extra pinch of salt if it is too sweet. Pipe or spread the frosting over the chocolate topping. Leftover prepared cupcakes can be stored covered tightly at room temperature for up to 3 days.

MAKE-AHEAD TIP: If you wish to prepare a day in advance, keep cupcakes covered tightly at room temperature and refrigerate frosting in an airtight container. Bring frosting to room temperature before spreading on cupcakes. Unfrosted cupcakes can be frozen up to 2 months; thaw overnight in the refrigerator and bring to room temperature before frosting and serving.

PEANUT BUTTER CUP ICE CREAM

Prep time: 30 minutes
Total time: 4–12 hours depending on the ice cream maker
Makes: 1 generous quart (1L)

Ingredients

2 large eggs

⅔ cup (133g) sugar

1 cup (240ml) whole milk

2 cups (475ml) heavy cream

½ cup (130g) creamy peanut butter

1½ cups (24 minis; 212g) chopped peanut butter cups

hot fudge sauce, for serving (optional)

Special Equipment

ice cream maker

Nothing is more satisfying than three generous scoops of ice cream on a hot summer afternoon. But imagine diving headfirst into a mountain of creamy homemade peanut butter ice cream packed with peanut butter cups. Things are about to get seriously delicious.

1   Whisk the eggs in a large mixing bowl until light and fluffy, about 1 minute. Whisk in the sugar until combined, then whisk in the milk and cream. Remove 1 cup of the mixture and pour into a medium-size mixing bowl. Whisk into that medium bowl the peanut butter until combined, then pour into the original large mixing bowl.

2   Transfer the mixture into an ice cream maker and churn according to the manufacturer's instructions. When ice cream is the consistency of soft-serve, quickly scoop into a freezer-safe airtight container and stir in the peanut butter cups until evenly distributed. Enjoy the soft ice cream now or cover and freeze for about 3 hours to yield a firmer texture. To serve, scoop ice cream into individual bowls and, if desired, drizzle with hot fudge.

MAKE-AHEAD TIP: For the best taste and texture, cover tightly and store ice cream in the freezer for no longer than 2 weeks. With ice cream this good, it won't even last that long!

 Sally Says: This homemade ice cream can be prepared in any 1-qt (1L) or higher ice cream maker. I simply use an ice cream maker attachment for my stand mixer.

MINT CHOCOLATE CREAM PIE

Prep time: 45 minutes
Total time: 6 hours, 45 minutes
Makes: 8 servings

Crust

20 Oreo® cookies (regular, Double Stuf, or any creme-filled chocolate cookie)

¼ cup (½ stick; 57g) unsalted butter, melted

Filling

2½ cups (590ml) whole milk

⅓ cup (67g) sugar

⅛ tsp salt

6 large egg yolks

2 tbsp cornstarch

6 tbsp butter (¾ stick; 85g), cut into 6 equal pieces

8oz semi-sweet chocolate, finely chopped

1 tsp vanilla extract

½ tsp peppermint extract

Topping

1 cup (240ml) cold heavy cream

1 tbsp confectioners' sugar

½ tsp vanilla extract

⅓ cup (60g) chopped Andes® Creme de Menthe Thins

Special Equipment

food processor or blender

9-in (23cm) pie dish

handheld or stand mixer fitted with a whisk attachment

Every time I've made my chocolate cream pie, guests leave happy with the written recipe in hand. The last time I made it, I decided to add peppermint extract and chopped Andes® mints. The chocolate filling is a cross between thick chocolate pudding and smooth custard. The top is covered with fresh whipped cream and, when chilled properly, the pie slices easily and neatly. If I'm going to use the word "addictive" to describe any recipe in this cookbook, it's this mint chocolate pie.

1   Preheat oven to 350°F (180°C).

2   Make the crust: In a food processor or blender, pulse the whole Oreos® into a fine crumb. Pour the cookie crumbs into a medium-size bowl and stir in melted butter until combined. Press the mixture evenly into the bottom and up the sides of a 9-in (23cm) pie dish. Use the bottom of a small glass or measuring cup to firmly press it down. Bake until the crust appears set, about 12–14 minutes. Remove from the oven and allow to cool in pie dish on a wire rack as you prepare the filling.

3   Make the filling: Combine the whole milk, sugar, and salt in a medium-size saucepan over medium heat. Whisk until all the sugar has dissolved, then bring to a gentle simmer, whisking occasionally.

4   Working quickly as the whole milk mixture begins to simmer, whisk the egg yolks and cornstarch together in a medium-size heatproof bowl until thick and smooth. Very slowly whisk in 1 cup (240ml) of the simmering whole milk mixture to slightly warm the egg yolk mixture. Then slowly whisk the egg yolk mixture into the remaining whole milk mixture in the saucepan. While continuing to slowly whisk, cook until the mixture is thick and big bubbles begin to burst on the surface. Remove pan from the heat and whisk in the butter, chocolate, and vanilla and peppermint extracts until completely smooth.

5   Pour filling into the cooled crust, smoothing the top with a rubber spatula. Place a sheet of plastic wrap on top of the surface and refrigerate until filling is set, about 4–6 hours.

6   Make the topping: When ready to serve the pie, with a handheld or stand mixer fitted with a whisk attachment, beat the cream, confectioners' sugar, and vanilla extract on low speed in a large bowl until combined, about 1 minute. Increase the speed to high and beat until soft peaks form, about 2–3 minutes. Spread whipped cream over pie and garnish with chopped Andes® mints. Use a sharp knife to make neat cuts and serve chilled.

MAKE-AHEAD TIP: The crust and filling can be prepared and assembled up to 4 days in advance. Cover tightly and store in the refrigerator. Prepare the whipped cream and garnish immediately before serving. Cover leftovers tightly and store in the refrigerator for up to 1 week.

DIRT 'N' GUMMY WORMS PARFAITS

Prep time: 7 hours
Total time: 7 hours
Makes: 6 parfaits

FILLING

2½ cups (590ml) whole milk

⅓ cup (67g) sugar

⅛ tsp salt

6 large egg yolks

2 tbsp cornstarch

6 tbsp butter (¾ stick; 85g),
cut into 6 equal pieces

8oz semi-sweet chocolate, finely
chopped

1 tsp vanilla extract

24 Oreos®

24 gummy worms

SPECIAL EQUIPMENT

food processor or blender

Dirt is a childhood favorite dessert combining gummy worms, crushed Oreos® (the dirt!), and a chocolate pudding mixture. I remember eating it at Halloween parties in grade school, where it was often served in a little faux flowerpot. Seriously, how cute is that? For these parfaits, I use the same chocolate filling recipe that I use in my Mint Chocolate Cream Pie (page 184). Gummy worms are an obvious necessity, making this a treat kids will love. I'm not embarrassed to say this thirty-year-old loves it, too. . . .

1   Make the filling: Combine the whole milk, sugar, and salt in a medium-size saucepan over medium heat. Whisk until all the sugar has dissolved, then bring to a gentle simmer, whisking occasionally.

2   Working quickly as the whole milk mixture begins to simmer, whisk the egg yolks and cornstarch together in a medium-size heatproof bowl until thick and smooth. Very slowly whisk in 1 cup (240ml) of the simmering whole milk mixture to slightly warm the egg yolk mixture. Then slowly whisk the egg yolk mixture into the remaining whole milk mixture in the saucepan. While continuing to slowly whisk, cook until the mixture is thick and big bubbles begin to burst on the surface. Remove pan from the heat and whisk in the butter, chocolate, and vanilla and peppermint extracts until completely smooth.

3   Pour the warm mixture into a large bowl. Place a sheet of plastic wrap on top of the surface of the filling and refrigerate until set, about 4–6 hours. Makes about 3 cups (852g).

4   Process the Oreos® in a food processor or blender until finely crushed. Once the chocolate pudding mixture has set, remove from the refrigerator and begin layering your parfaits. Layer 2 tablespoons of crushed Oreos®, then ½ cup (142g) of the chocolate pudding mixture, then 2 more tablespoons of crushed Oreos®. Top each with 4 gummy worms. Serve cold.

MAKE-AHEAD TIP: These are great make-ahead treats for parties. Prep the filling up to 3 days in advance, keeping it tightly covered in the refrigerator until ready to use. Assemble the parfaits up to 4–5 hours in advance. Any longer than that, the bottom layer of crushed Oreos® will get soggy.

BUTTERFINGER® SCOTCHEROOS

Prep time: 30 minutes
Total time: 2 hours, 30 minutes
Makes: 16 bars

INGREDIENTS

1 cup (240ml) honey

1 cup plus 1 tbsp (274g) creamy peanut butter, divided

1 cup (240g) butterscotch morsels, divided

4½ cups (113g) crispy rice cereal

1 cup (125g) chopped Butterfinger® candy bars (5–6 fun-size bars), divided

½ cup (91g) milk chocolate chips

SPECIAL EQUIPMENT

9-in (23cm) square baking pan

Scotcheroos are no-bake treats combining butterscotch morsels, peanut butter, and chocolate—fun to make, delicious to eat, and enjoyable to say. In my opinion, they're the perfect dessert for Butterfinger® candy bars. This recipe is my version of the scotcheroo—heavy on the peanut butter, generous with the butterscotch, and overloaded on candy bars. These treats are crispy, chewy, chocolaty, dense—and you need to make them right now.

1   Line a 9-in (23cm) square baking pan with aluminum foil or parchment paper, leaving enough overhang on the sides to easily remove the bars after they have chilled. Set aside.

2   Melt the honey, 1 cup (258g) peanut butter, and ½ cup (120g) butterscotch morsels together in a medium saucepan over low-medium heat. Stir constantly with a heatproof rubber spatula or wooden spoon until smooth, about 5 minutes. Remove from heat and stir in the cereal and half of the chopped candy bars until combined. The chocolate on the candy bars will melt—this is okay!

3   Spoon mixture into the prepared pan and use a rubber spatula to firmly press the mixture into the pan. The key is to press firmly so the bars are dense and retain their shape when cut. Set aside.

4   Combine the remaining 1 tablespoon peanut butter, ½ cup (120g) butterscotch morsels, and the chocolate chips in a small heatproof bowl. Melt in the microwave on 50 percent power in 20-second increments, stirring after each increment, until completely smooth and melted. Spread evenly over cereal bars. Sprinkle with remaining chopped candy bars.

5   Cover tightly with aluminum foil or plastic wrap, then refrigerate for at least 2 hours. Once chilled, remove from the pan using the overhang on the sides, invert onto cutting board, peel away foil, and cut into squares.

MAKE-AHEAD TIP: Store the bars in an airtight container at room temperature for up to 1 week. To freeze, place bars in layers separated by parchment or wax paper in airtight container. Freeze for up to 1 month; let stand at room temperature for 1 hour before serving.

INDEX